BEAR COLORING BOOK

30 HAND DRAWN, DOODLE AND FOLK ART STYLE LOVE TEDDY BEAR ADULT COLORING DESIGNS

BY
LOUISE FORD

ISBN-13: 978-1539083535
ISBN-10: 1539083535

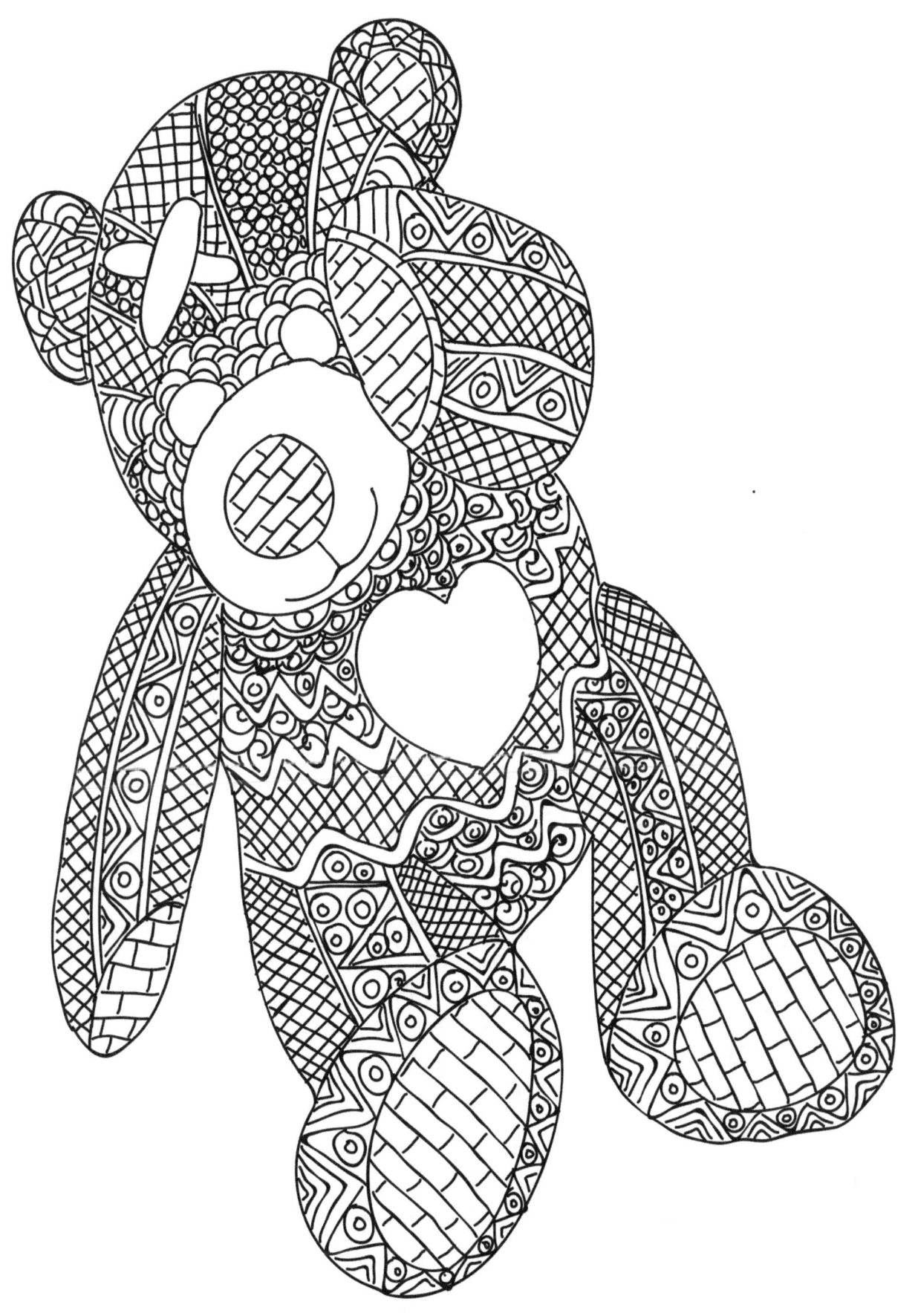

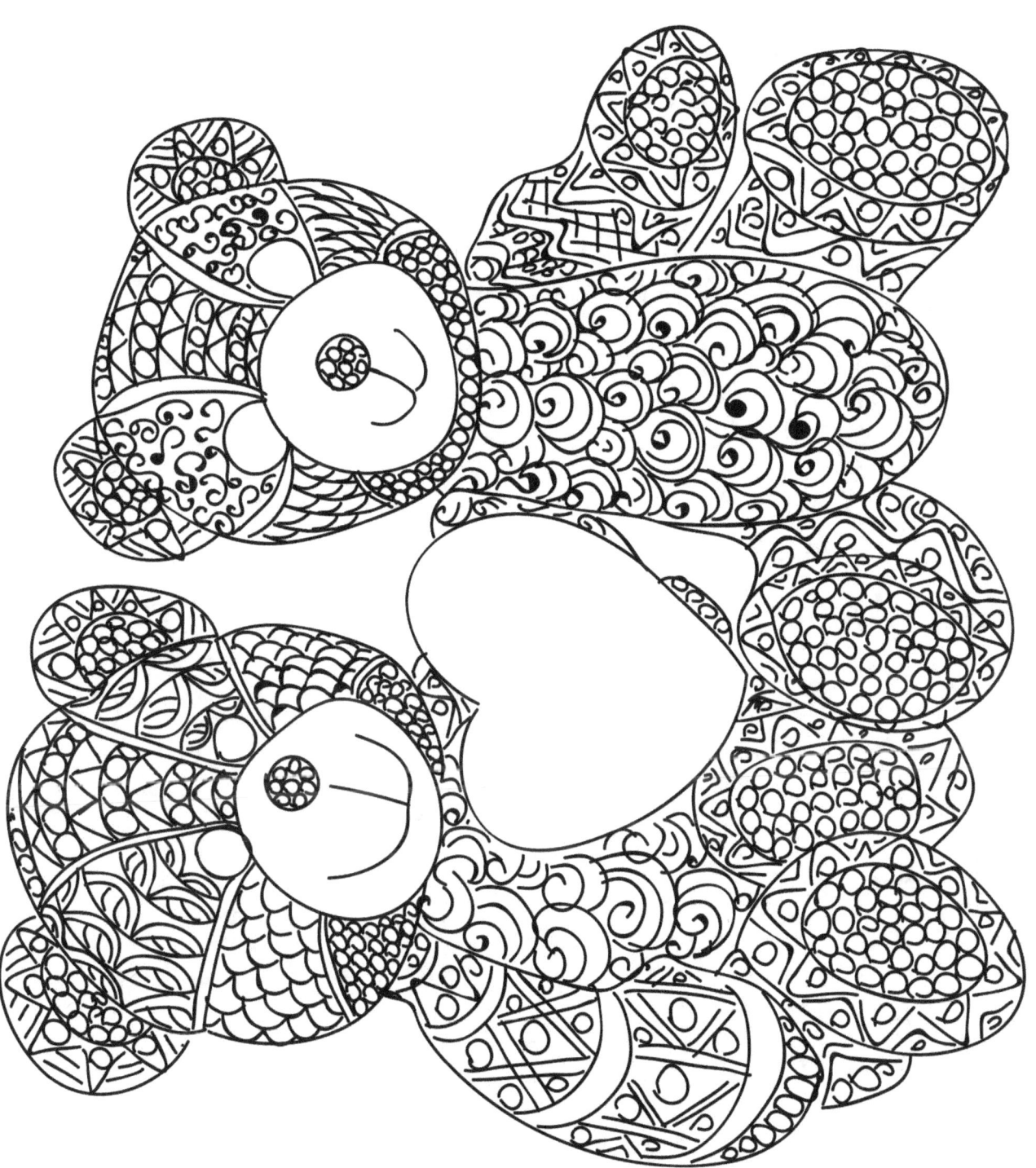

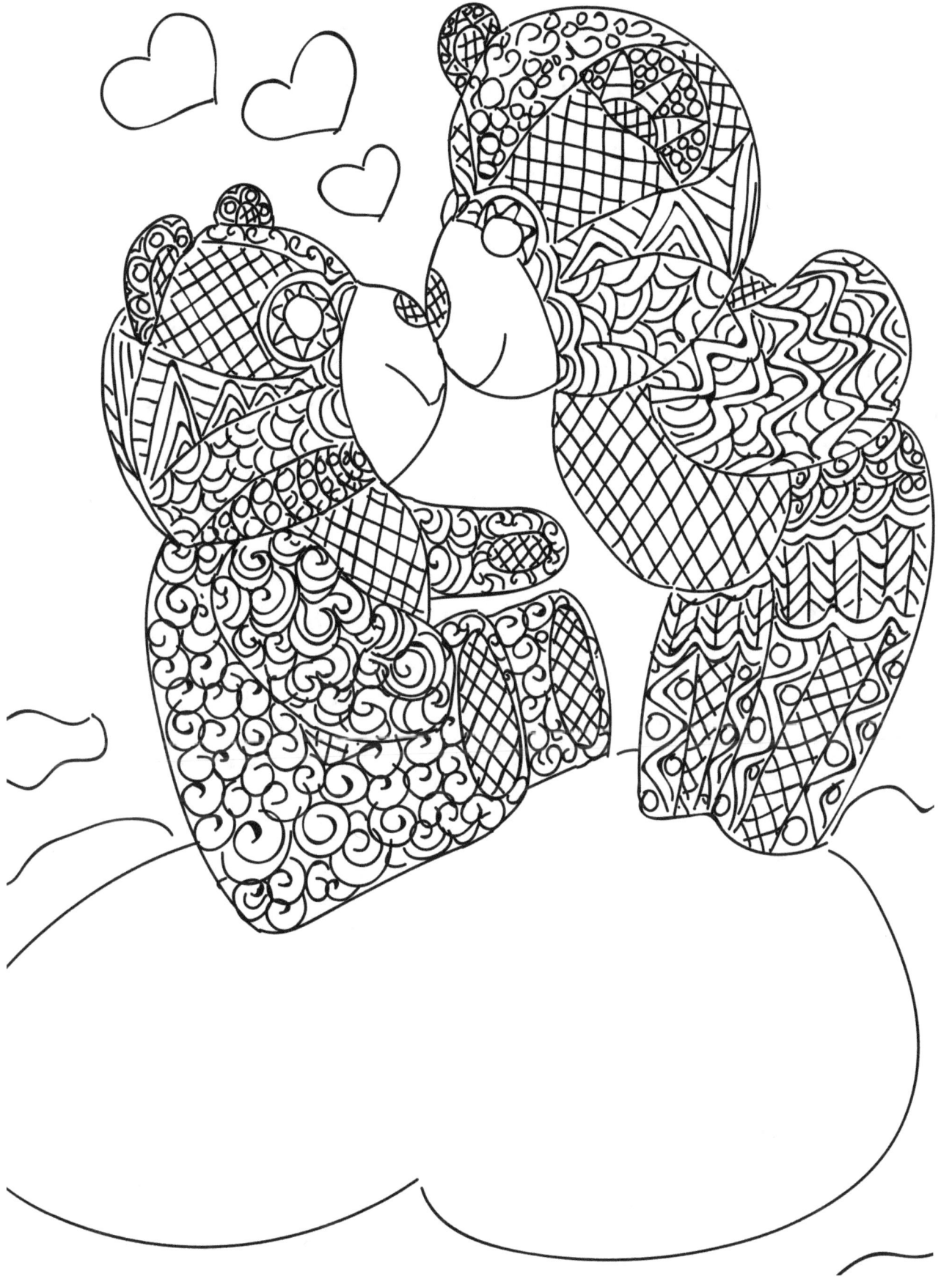

www.ingramcontent.com/pod-product-compliance
Lightning Source LLC
Chambersburg PA
CBHW081858280526
45789CB00007B/2758